JANUA LINGUARUM

STUDIA MEMORIAE
NICOLAI VAN WIJK DEDICATA

edenda curat

C. H. VAN SCHOONEVELD

Indiana University

Series Minor, 105

THE METHODOLOGICAL STATUS OF GRAMMATICAL ARGUMENTATION

by

RUDOLF P. BOTHA

1970

MOUTON

THE HAGUE · PARIS

LIBRARY OF CONGRES CATALOG CARD NUMBER : 79 — 126050

Printed in The Netherlands by Mouton & Co., Printers, The Hague.

PREFACE

The present volume contains a preliminary report on the findings of a not yet completed analysis of the methodological role that grammatical argumentation plays in transformational generative grammar. As this study is, to my knowledge, the first systematic attempt to treat this topic, the conclusions it contains are not final.

Various scholars have contributed to the clarification of the views that I hold on the subject of grammatical argumentation. In particular, I would like to express my gratitude to Professor H. Schultink of the University of Utrecht and Professor W. Kempen of the University of Stellenbosch for their critical comments on earlier versions of the manuscript. Other scholars whom I would like to thank for their willingness to participate in discussions of the topics treated in the present volume are A. Evers, A. Kraak and H. Brandt-Corstius. Comments that they made at a meeting of the Dutch Linguistic Society in February, 1969 helped to clarify a number of points which I had formulated inadequately at that time.

Finally I am grateful to Mrs. J. Degenaar and Mrs. S. Conradie for the most efficient way in which they typed the various versions of the manuscript of this monograph.

Stellenbosch, R.P.B.
October 1969.

CONTENTS

INTRODUCTION

1.1 GENERAL REMARKS

Transformational generative grammar has enriched modern linguistics in two fundamental ways. Firstly, reviving and refining ideas of great scholars such as the Port-Royal grammarians and the Cartesians, it presents a radically different conception of the essential properties of natural language, emphasising its innovative character, its freedom from stimulus control, and its coherence and appropriateness to the situation (cf. Chomsky, 1968: 11). Secondly, transformational generative grammar has introduced into modern linguistics a new set of scientific standards for judging the correctness and significance of grammatical and linguistic claims. In order to be able to meet these new scientific criteria, transformational generative grammar has also provided modern linguistics with new modes and patterns of argumentation on both the linguistic and the grammatical level.

More and more present-day linguists and grammarians concede the inescapability of the general methodological maxim that the correctness of the results of linguistic and grammatical analyses depends on the validity of the modes and patterns of argumentation by means of which they are reached. The corollary of this concession is that it is an imperious necessity that the validity of these modes and patterns of reasoning must be thoroughly checked and rechecked. This study aims at assessing the limits on the general validity of one of the methodological instruments of transformational generative grammar: grammatical argumentation. The conclusions presented in this volume are the first tentative results of a more extensive, and still unfinished, analysis of the anatomy of linguistic and grammatical inquiry. It is to be expected that, as this larger analysis is extended with respect to its scope and depth, some of these tentative results would have to be mod fied and others rejected.

1.2 THEORETICAL BACKGROUND

The questions that are considered in this study can be formulated the most explicitly against the background of the 'minimal' goal of a generative grammar. The 'minimal' goal of a generative grammar has two, closely related, aspects (cf. Chomsky, 1957: 13-13; Bach, 1964: 13):

(i) A generative grammar must enumerate by means of a finite set of rules all and only the grammatical sentences of a language.

(ii) It must assign a structural description to each of the enumerated sentences.[1]

The assignment of structural descriptions to sentences takes place at various structural levels: the level of syntactic structure, the level of phonological structure, and the level of semantic structure. Each of these structural levels is constituted by sublevels. The level of syntactic structure consists, for example, of the levels of deep and surface structure. The level of deep structure, in turn, is constituted by relational, categorial, selectional and lexical structure. It is therefore obvious that a first major concern of the grammarian is to determine the structural description that must

---

[1] This goal is in two respects 'minimal': (i) It can be required that a grammar also specifies in which respect ungrammatical sentences are deviant (cf. Katz, 1964a; Seuren, 1969: §§ 1.4.4 and 3.2.2). (ii) Furthermore the condition can be imposed on a grammar that it must be mentalistic, i.e., that it must have psychological relevance (cf. Katz, 1964b; Botha, 1968: § 3.5).

be assigned to each generated sentence at each structural level. A second major concern of his is to formulate the rules which generate these structural descriptions. In this study I shall deal mainly with the first task of the grammarian, viz. assigning structural descriptions to sentences.

Since grammar is an empirical science within the framework of transformational generative grammar, the structural descriptions which the grammarian assigns to sentences must bear an empirical nature. An empirical science aims, by definition, at making true statements by way of formulating testable hypotheses (cf. Bunge, 1959: 44-45). The truth of an empirical hypothesis is determined by checking against independent evidence whether its consequences, i.e., the predictions that can be derived from it, are correct (cf. Hempel, 1965: 3). The independent evidence must meet the condition that its correctness has been established on an intersubjective level (cf. Bunge, 1959: 81). An empirical statement is CONFIRMED if it is supported by such independent evidence, is DISCONFIRMED if it is in conflict with such evidence, and is UNCONFIRMED if, for practical reasons, it is impossible to obtain such supporting or conflicting evidence (cf. Hempel, 1965: 3-4). The grammarian who assigns a given structural description SD_1 to a sentence S must face the grammatical confirmation problem in the sense that he must demonstrate why SD_1, and not one of the possible alternative structural descriptions $SD_2., .., SD_x$, is the correct structural description for S.[2] Looking back upon the development which transformational generative grammar has undergone during the past decade, it appears that grammarians have approached the problem of demonstrating the correctness of structural descriptions along two different lines.

The first line of approach — which is characteristic of the earlier phase of development of transformational generative grammar — can be labelled 'indirect'. It implies that grammarians assign in a more or less intuitive, and sometimes outright arbitrary, way a

---

[2] A grammarian must also face a second aspect of the grammatical confirmation problem, viz. demonstrating the correctness of the grammatical rules that he formulates.

structural description to a sentence. Little or no attention is given in this approach to advancing arguments in justification of particular structural descriptions that are assigned to particular sentences. In this line of approach grammarians are primarily concerned with determining and formalising the grammatical rules that must generate these sentences and their structural descriptions. Arguments are provided mainly to justify these rules, and not to support the structural descriptions which they generate. The assumption is that, if the rules which generate, and therefore generalise, these structural descriptions are correct, then the structural descriptions are correct too. The rules are considered to be correct if their predictions about the grammatical properties — such as grammaticalness, syntactic homonymity, syntactic relatedness, etc. — of unobserved but generated sentences are confirmed by independent evidence. The independent evidence is constituted by the linguistic intuitions of native speakers (cf., e.g., Bach, 1964: 181-182, 184-185; Botha, 1968: 63-64, 73). The indirectness of this approach consists in the fact that the problem of the correctness of structural descriptions is tackled via the problem of the correctness of grammatical rules. Lees' (1959) monograph on English nominalizations is a typical illustration of the indirect approach. In this monograph Lees is primarily concerned with formulating and explicating the rules that generate English nominalizations and their structural descriptions, and to a far lesser extent with justifying directly the assignment of particular structural descriptions to particular types of nominalizations. A concrete example of the manifestation of this indirect approach is the attention that grammarians gave to formulating the passive transformation, and their correlating lack of interest in giving a direct justification for the structural description assigned to the strings which constituted the domain of this transformation (cf., e.g., Chomsky, 1957: 42-43, 77-81).

The second line of approach — which is typical of the present phase of development of transformational generative grammar — is the 'direct' one, the one of grammatical argumentation. In this line of approach the emphasis is on providing grammatical arguments for or against assigning a particular structural description to a particular sentence. Grammarians who take this line of approach to the problem of demonstrating the correctness of structural descriptions often do not even attempt to formulate the rules that must generate the sentences and their structural descriptions. Underlying this approach is the assumption that grammatical argumentation is a methodologically valid way of demonstrating the correctness or incorrectness of specific structural descriptions. The approach of grammatical argumentation is illustrated beautifully by Lakoff's treatment of instrumental adverbs in English.

1.3 LAKOFF ON GRAMMATICAL ARGUMENTATION

The questions which Lakoff discusses in his paper "Instrumental Adverbs and the Concept of Deep Structure" exist on three different levels. On the linguistic level Lakoff poses the question as to whether the conditions (1)(i)-(iv) that Chomsky (1965) and Katz and Postal (1964) impose on deep structure define only a single level of linguistic structure. An alternative view is that these four conditions define two, three or even four different levels of linguistic structure.

(1)(i) "Basic grammatical relations (e.g., subject-of, object-of) are represented at this level in terms of fundamental grammatical categories (e.g., S, NP, VP, N, V)."

(ii) "The correct generalizations about selectional restrictions and co-occurrence can be stated at this level."

(iii) "Lexical items are assigned to their appropriate categories at this level."

(iv) "The structures defined at this level are the input to the transformational rules." (Lakoff, 1968: 4).

Lakoff's conclusions, and especially the correctness of his conclusions, concerning the number of linguistic levels that are defined by (1)(i)-(iv) are not discussed in this study. The pattern of argumentation that Lakoff uses to support these conclusions is the objec: of an analysis of the structure of linguistic argumentation, and not of grammatical argumentation.

On the second level, the grammatical level, Lakoff considers the quest_on as to whether instrumental adverbs can be viewed against the background of (1)(i)-(iv) as constituting a deep structure categ>ry in English. This question he transposes on the third level into a grammatical problem concerning specific English sente¬ces: Does the prepositional object *with a knife* constitute, as ar instrumental adverb, in the sentence (2) a deep structure element, or do the conditions (1)(i)-(iv) force the grammarian to assign to (2) the same deep structure as to (3), a deep structure in which the category 'instrumental adverb' is no constituent?

(2)   *Seymour sliced the salami with a knife*

(3)   *Seymour used a knife to slice the salami*[3]

The existence of this concrete grammatical problem is suggested by the incidental observation that (2) and (3) are synonymous on the level of their semantic interpretation (cf. Lakoff, 1968: 7).

According to Lakoff (p. 6) transformationalists, following the tradi:ion, have assigned to (2) and (3) non-identical deep structures. The deep structure (4), containing the constituent 'instrumental adverb', has been assigned to (2); the deep structure (5), not containing the constituent 'instrumental adverb', to (3).

(4)

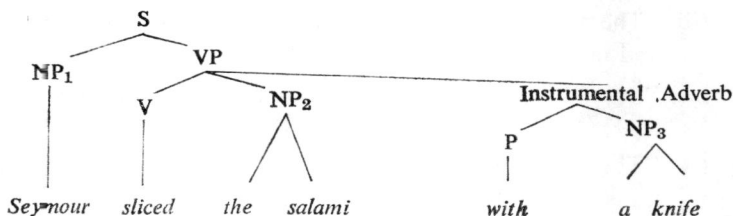

---

[3] Further examples of instrumental adverbs, which Lakoff presents, are the prepcsitional objects *with a sliderule, with dynamite, with the Russian spy, with a bat* in respectively (i) *Albert computed the answer with a sliderule* (ii) *John killea Harry with dynamite* (iii) *James Bond broke the window with the Russian spy* (v) *I broke the window with a bat.*

(5)

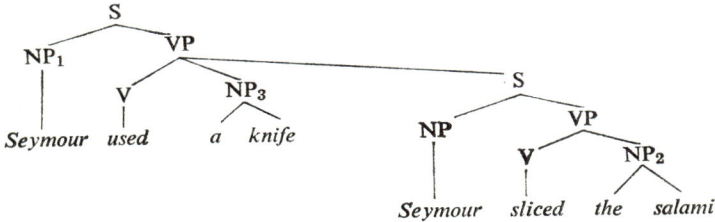

The grammatical constructions in (2) and (3) can also be indicated by, respectively, (6) and (7) (cf. Lakoff, 1968: 7).

(6) $NP_1 - V - NP_2 - $ with $ - NP_3$

(7) $NP_1 - $ use $ - NP_3 - $ to $ - V - NP_2$

The grammatical problem that Lakoff treats concerns the identity of the deep structures of sentences which have different superficial structures. Lakoff's conclusion is that (2) and (3) must be assigned the same deep structure, the deep structure (5). He accordingly asserts that the category 'instrumental adverb' is no constituent in the deep structure of (2), and he, furthermore, claims that this category does not constitute a deep structure category in English at all (cf. pp. 5-7, 22-24). In order to prove the correctness of his claims about the deep structure that must be assigned to (2) and (3) Lakoff provides a number of GRAMMATICAL ARGUMENTS. He makes no attempt to formulate and formalise the rules which must generate the given deep structure. This is to say that he does not approach the problem of demonstrating the correctness of structural descriptions along the indirect way of formulating rules, and checking the correctness of these rules, but along the direct way of grammatical argumentation.

On his approach to this problem Lakoff offers the following

illuminating remarks: "Due to the nature of the definition of
deep structure, one can provide arguments for IDENTITY of deep
structures without proposing what those deep structures are and
without proposing any transformational derivations. This type of
argument differs considerably from the type of argument that has
been used in transformational research so far. To date, research
in transformational grammar has been oriented toward proposing
rules. Arguments concerning generalizations of deep structure
selectional restrictions and co-occurrences have been brought up
only in support of some given set of rules. What we have done
is to show that arguments of this sort can be used by themselves
without discussion of rules at all" (p. 24).

1.4   THE METHODOLOGICAL QUESTIONS

Against the theoretical background outlined in § 1.2 and Lakoff's
views on grammatical argumentation presented in § 1.3 the general
methodological questions that will be considered in this study
can now be formulated. It has become clear that present-day
grammarians approach the problem of the demonstration of the
correctness of structural descriptions along two different lines.
The first approach of the grammatical confirmation problem, i.e.,
the indirect one, is based on the standard methodological practice
of formulating rules and testing the correctness of the predictions
that can be derived from these rules. The second approach, i.e.,
the direct one, is that of grammatical argumentation, as used by
Lakoff and many other contemporary grammarians.[4] The general
methodological questions to be considered in the present volume
are :
  (i) Does grammatical argumentation constitute a methodologi-

[4] Loss is another leading transformationalist who holds this point of view.
Consider, for example, his paper "On Declarative Sentences" (in press). In
it he produces a series of grammatical arguments to show that a declarative
sentence such as (v) must not be derived from a deep structure such as (vi),

cally valid solution to the problem of confirming or dis-
confirming hypotheses about structural descriptions?[5]

(ii) Should grammatical argumentation be found to be a methodologically invalid solution to the grammatical confirmation problem, would it then have methodologically fruitful
functions in grammatical analysis at all?

---

but from a deep structure such as (vii) that contains the constituent 'perfor-
mative verb'.

(v) *Prices slumped*

(vi)

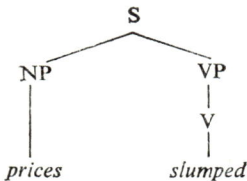

(vii)

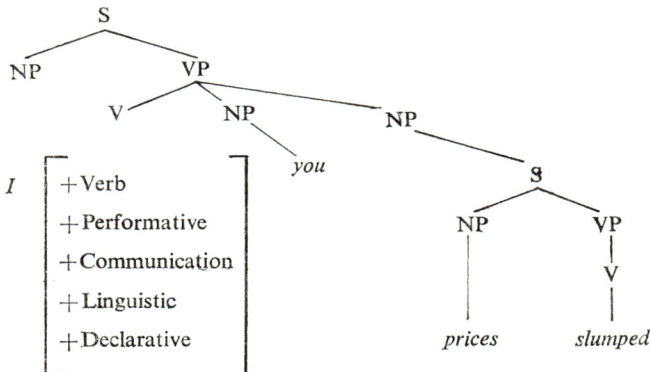

[5] A question which is analogous to this one — but which is not considered
in this study — is the following one: Does grammatical argumentation constitute a methodologically valid solution to the problem of confirming or dis-
confirming proposed grammatical rules?

These questions concern the scope within which grammatical
argumentation is a methodologically valid instrument in grammatical analysis. In order to answer them in a fully motivated way,
it is necessary first to give attention to the following topics:

    (i) the logical structure of a well-formed argument,

   (ii) the structure of a number of typical grammatical arguments,
       and

  (iii) the methodological principles determining the abstract
       structure of grammatical argumentation.

2

THE LOGICAL STRUCTURE OF AN ARGUMENT

An argument can be regarded, in a rather informal way, as a methodological instrument which has the function of supporting or contradicting a claim or conclusion. For the purpose of this investigation I consider Toulmin's analysis of the structure of an argument quite illuminating. Although Toulmin (1964) is primarily concerned with the structure of the arguments of jurisprudence, many of his conclusions about the structure of arguments are also valid for the arguments encountered in empirical science.

According to Toulmin a well-formed argument has the following components :

   (i) a claim or conclusion,

   (ii) data,

   (iii) a warrant,

   (iv) a qualifier,

   (v) conditions of rebuttal, and

   (vi) a backing.

The nature and function of each of these components can be indicated by considering one of Toulmin's examples of a well-formed argument.

Every argument has a CLAIM or CONCLUSION of which the correctness or incorrectness is affirmed or denied. The claim (8) is a typical example of this component of an argument.

(8)   Harry is a British subject

The DATA are the so-called facts which are provided to support or contradict the claim or conclusion. In support of (8) the datum (9) can be provided.

(9)   Harry was born in Bermuda

Next a rule or 'inference-licence' must be given to show why the data can be taken as supporting or contradicting the claim or conclusion. The component of an argument that has the function of authorising the inference of the claim or conclusion from the data is called the WARRANT. A warrant is a bridge-like, hypothetical statement that has the form: If X, then Y. (10) can be taken as the warrant authorising the inference of the claim (8) from the datum (9).

(10)   If a man was born in Bermuda, then he will be a British subject

It is possible to distinguish between different types of warrants, not all of which confer the same degree of force on the conclusion which they authorise. Some warrants allow us to accept the claim or conclusion unequivocally, others authorise only a tentative step to be taken from the data to the claim or conclusion. In order to specify explicitly the degree of force which the data confer on the claim or conclusion by virtue of the warrant, a fourth component is built into an argument: the QUALIFIER. Usually modal expressions such as *definitely, necessarily, presumably, probably,* etc. function as qualifiers in arguments. The claim (8) can be reformulated as the qualified claim (11).

(11)   Harry is *presumably* a British subject

When a particular qualifier is used in an argument to modify the claim, it becomes necessary to give the reasons for using it. This is done by incorporating into the argument a fifth component, the CONDITIONS OF REBUTTAL. The conditions of rebuttal specify the circumstances under which the warrant is invalid, i.e., when its authority must be set aside. To motivate the use of the qualifier *presumably* in (11) the conditions of rebuttal (12)(i) and (ii) can be built into the argument.

(12) (i) Unless his parents were aliens
     (ii) Unless he has become a naturalised American

Under these conditions the warrant (10) does not authorise that the step from the datum (9) to the claim or conclusion (8) be taken.

Even if the data, warrant, qualifier, and conditions of rebuttal were specified explicitly in an argument, a sceptic could still refuse to accept that the claim or conclusion is correct. It is not sufficient only to know under which particular conditions the warrant is invalid. It must also be known why a warrant is in general valid. This is to say that the grounds from which a warrant derives its general validity must also be specified explicitly in an argument. These grounds that validate a warrant in a general way are presented in the sixth component of an argument, the BACKING. (13) can be taken as the backing from which the warrant (10) derives its general validity.

(13)   The British and Bermudan statutes and legal provisions A, B, C, and D specify that a man born in Bermuda will be a British subject

Unlike warrants, backings are not hypothetical, bridge-like statements. Backings have the form of categorical assertions of fact. The role that backings play in arguments differs from that of data. If there is to be an argument at all, data of some kind must be presented. A conclusion or claim for which the supporting data are not presented explicitly, will not be accepted. Often however a claim will be accepted even if the backing in the argument is not specified. Some warrants are accepted provisionally without further challenge.

The "Harry argument" can be represented schematically as (14).

(14)

DATA:		CLAIM/CONCLUSION:
Harry was born in Bermuda.	→ *So, presumably,*	Harry is a British subject.

WARRANT:	CONDITIONS OF REBUTTAL:
Since	*Unless*
If a man was born in Bermuda, then he will be a British subject.	(i) His parents were aliens, (ii) He has become a naturalised American.

BACKING :

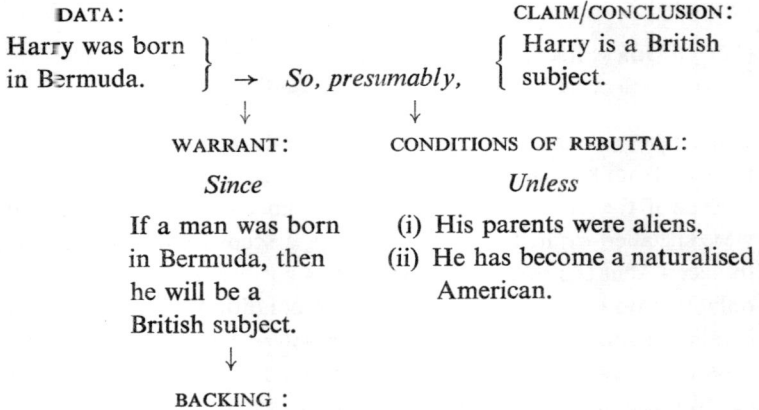

On account of the fact that
The British and Bermudan statutes and
legal provisions A, B, C, and D specify
that a man born in Bermuda will be a
British subject.

Since the conclusions of well-formed arguments are not necessarily true, the distinction between well-formed arguments with
true conclusions and well-formed arguments with false conclusions
is crucial (cf., e.g., Toulmin, 1964: 135; Clark and Welsch, 1962:
35; Salmon, 1963: 18). In order to qualify as well-formed an
argument must meet two conditions. Firstly, it must be possible
to present all its components explicitly. Secondly, these components must be related in the proper way. In order to have a true
conclusion, an argument must not only meet these two conditions
of well-formedness, but must also satisfy a third condition. The
third condition requires that the statements which present the data,
backing and conditions of rebuttal of the argument must be true
statements. For example,

(i) if Harry was not born in Bermuda, i.e., if the statement
that presents the datum in (14) is false, or

(ii) if the statutes and legal provisions A, B, C, and D do not exist or have a different content, i.e., if the statement that presents the backing in (14) is false, or

(iii) if a person can at the same time be a British and an American subject or if he can be British even if his parents are aliens, i.e., if the statements presenting the conditions of rebuttal are false,

then the conclusion that Harry is presumably a British subject is false.[1]

It is now possible to proceed to an analysis of the structure of a number of typical grammatical arguments that are provided in justification of structural descriptions.

---

[1] The distinction between well-formed arguments with true and well-formed arguments with false conclusions will crop up again in § 5.3.

THE STRUCTURE OF A TYPICAL GRAMMATICAL ARGUMENT

3.1 GENERAL REMARKS

A number of the arguments which Lakoff (1968) presents will be analyzed to illustrate the structure of a typical grammatical argument. Lakoff advances these arguments to prove the correctness of the grammatical claims (15)(i) and (ii).

(15) (i) Sentences (2) and (3) have an identical deep structure.
 (ii) The deep structure that must be assigned to (2) and (3) is (5), i.e., the deep structure in which the category 'instrumental adverb' is no constituent.

Notice that Lakoff does not present the components of all his arguments equally explicitly. It is in many cases difficult to find out precisely what are the warrants and backings of his arguments. This fact must, however, not obscure the point that with a little patience these inexplicit components of his arguments can be brought to the surface.

3.2 THE FIRST MAIN ARGUMENT

The data in the argument whose claim is (15)(i) — i.e., that (2) and (3) have an identical deep structure — are presented in the statement that the constructions in (2) and (3) are in a one-to-one correspondence with respect to a number of grammatical characteristics (p. 7). These grammatical characteristics are those suggested by the conditions (1)(i)-(iv) on deep structure: relational, selectional, lexical and transformational characteristics. The warrant in this argument of Lakoff's is the following: If two sentences are constituted by constructions which are in a one-to-one correspondence with respect to relational, selectional, lexical and transformational characteristics, then they have an identical deep structure. In this argument the backing is the following: A grammar must explicitly present linguistically significant generalizations (p. 7). This backing implies that linguistic facts that are the same must be presented as the same, that facts that are related must be presented as related, etc. This grammatical argument of Lakoff's can be represented schematically as (16).

(16)

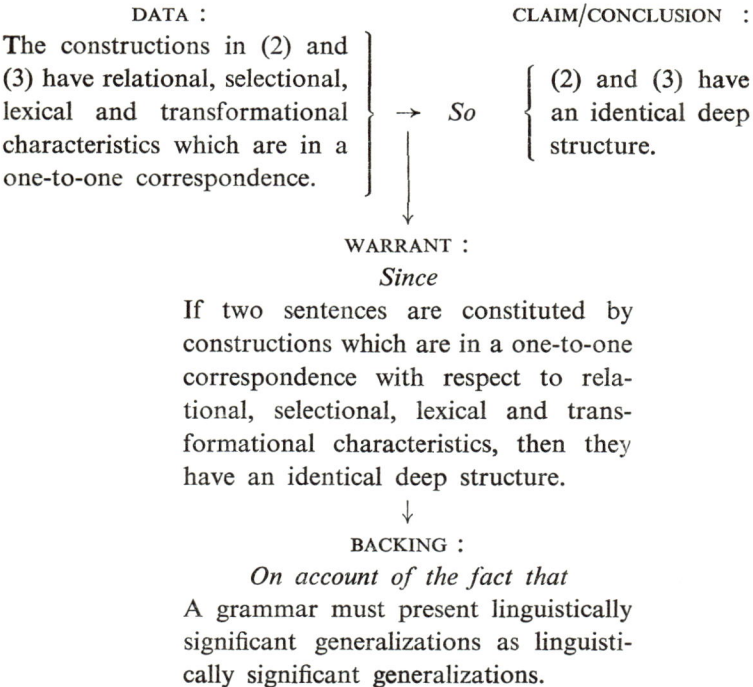

DATA :

The constructions in (2) and (3) have relational, selectional, lexical and transformational characteristics which are in a one-to-one correspondence.

→ *So*

CLAIM/CONCLUSION :

(2) and (3) have an identical deep structure.

WARRANT :
Since
If two sentences are constituted by constructions which are in a one-to-one correspondence with respect to relational, selectional, lexical and transformational characteristics, then they have an identical deep structure.

BACKING :
On account of the fact that
A grammar must present linguistically significant generalizations as linguistically significant generalizations.

In the grammatical argument (16) a number of interesting features of the abstract pattern of grammatical argumentation are realised. Firstly, note that in (16) the qualifier and the conditions of rebuttal are not explicitly presented. From this fact it is clear that Lakoff considers the claim or conclusion in (16) to be correct in an unqualified way. This is to say that the qualifier "necessarily" should be read in this claim.

Notice, secondly, that the data in (16) are not presented in terms of a protocol sentence, but in terms of a hypothesis. A protocol sentence, on the one hand, refers directly to data that can in one way or another be observed or perceived. The correctness of a protocol sentence can accordingly be determined by confronting it directly with observational data (cf. Caws, 1965: 73ff.). A hypothesis, on the other hand, does not refer directly to observational or perceptual data. It, however, has at least one consequence that refers directly to data of an observational nature. A hypothesis can therefore not be tested by confronting it directly with observational data, but is testable in the sense that its consequences can be confronted with such data (cf. Caws, 1965: 79). Within the framework of transformational generative grammar the only data that qualify as observational data are the data about the perceptual aspect of linguistic utterances, and the linguistic intuitions of native speakers about their grammatical properties (cf., e.g., Bach, 1964: 3-4; Botha, 1968: 70-71). It is obvious that the grammatical characteristics — relational, selectional, lexical and transformational — used as the data in (16) are neither perceptual nor intuitive phenomena.[1] The correctness of the statement that presents the data in (16) can therefore not be tested by confronting it directly with either perceptual or intuitive data. In order to demonstrate the correctness of this statement, Lakoff is therefore forced to give further grammatical arguments. The statement that presents the data in (16) constitutes the claim or conclusion of these new arguments. The function of these arguments is to anchor the statement presenting the data in (16) in observational evidence.

[1]   These data are not so-called 'primary linguistic data'. Cf. note 5 of § 4.

3.3 SUPPORTING ARGUMENTS

In order to extend our exemplification of the structure of a typical grammatical argument, let us consider a few of the arguments which Lakoff advances in order to establish the correctness of the statement presenting the data in (16). These arguments must prove the correctness of the claim about the one-to-one relationship between the relational, selectional, lexical and transformational characteristics of the constructions in (2) and (3). Since Lakoff has little to say about the correspondence in lexical characteristics, I shall not give further attention to it. Because of its length and intricacy Lakoff's argument to demonstrate the correspondence in transformational characteristics is not repeated here (cf. Lakoff, 1968: 21-23). Only two of his arguments concerning the one-to-one correspondence of respectively selectional and relational characteristics are considered.

The claim of the first series of new arguments provided by Lakoff is that the constructions in (2), represented by (6), and (3), represented by (7), have selectional characteristics which are in a one-to-one correspondence. The first of this series of arguments has as its claim the statement that the verbs in the corresponding constructions both have the selectional feature [+ Activity]. As data Lakoff presents the observations that the replacement of the corresponding verbs by verbs with the selectional feature [— Activity] causes both (2) and (3) to become ungrammatical. Instead of illustrating the latter observation with respect to (2) and (3) Lakoff does it with regard to (17)(i), which can be represented as (6), and (18)(i), which can be represented as (7) (cf. pp. 13-14 of Lakoff's paper).

(17) (i) *Albert* computed *the answer with a sliderule*
   (ii) *Albert knew *the answer with a sliderule*

(18) (i) *Albert used a sliderule to* compute *the answer*
   (ii) **Albert used a sliderule to* know *the answer*

In (17)(i) and (18)(i) the verb *compute* has the selectional feature [+ Activity], whereas in (17)(ii) and (18)(ii) the verb *know* has the

selectional feature [— Activity]. The warrant in this argument
of Lakoff's is presumably the following: If the same grammatical
modification of two constructions has the same effect on their
grammaticalness, then this modification has affected a grammatical characteristic which these constructions share. This argument
can be represented schematically as (19).

(19)

DATA: CLAIM/CONCLUSION:

The replacement of the corresponding verbs in (2) — or (17)
(i) — and (3) — or (18)(i) —
with verbs which have the
selectional feature [— Activity]   → *So*
causes both (2) — or (17)(i) —
and (3) — or (18)(i) — to become
ungrammatical.

The given correspond-
ing constructions in
(2) — or (17)(i) —
and (3) — or (18)(i) —
share the selectional
feature [+ Activity].

WARRANT :
Since
If the same grammatical modification of two
constructions has the same effect on their
grammaticalness, then this modification has
affected a grammatical characteristic which
these constructions share.

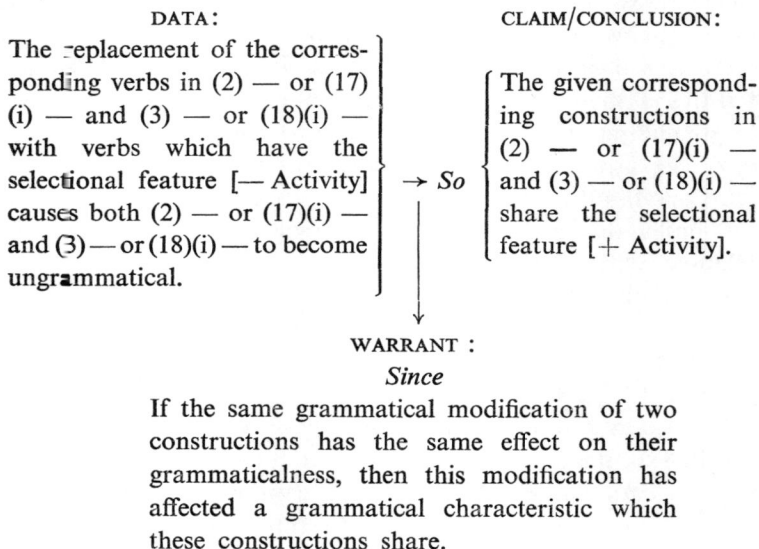

With respect to (19) observe firstly that Lakoff does not only
fail to present explicitly the qualifier and conditions of rebuttal,
but also the warrant and its backing. The significance of the
absence of the backing will be commented on in § 5.3. Secondly,
note that the data in (19) are presented by a protocol sentence.
This protocol sentence refers directly to an intuitive phenomenon:
the grammaticalness of sentences.

The second series of new arguments that Lakoff provides in
justification of the statement presenting the data in (16) has the
specific claim that (2) and (3) exhibit relational characteristics
that correspond in a one-to-one fashion. As the data in the first

of these arguments Lakoff presents the statement that the grammatical transposition of (2) and (3) into the interrogative form
affects the semantic interpretation of (2) and (3) in the same way.
In both (20), the interrogative form of (2), and (21), the interrogative form of (3), what is being questioned is not whether the
slicing took place, but whether the instrument that was used was
a knife (cf. Lakoff, 1968: 17-18).

(20)   *Did Seymour slice the salami with a knife?*

(21)   *Did Seymour use a knife to slice the salami?*

The warrant in this argument is presumably the following one:
If the same grammatical modification of two sentences affects
their respective semantic interpretations in the same way, then
shared grammatical relations exist between the constituents of
these sentences. Schematically this argument can be presented
as (22).

(22)

DATA :

The grammatical transposition
of (2) and (3) into the interrogative form has the same → *So*
effect on their semantic interpretation.

CLAIM/CONCLUSION :

Corresponding gram-
matical relations exist
between the consti-
tuents in (2) and (3).

WARRANT :
Since
If the same grammatical modification of two
sentences has the same effect on their semantic
interpretation, then corresponding grammatical
relations exist between their constituents.

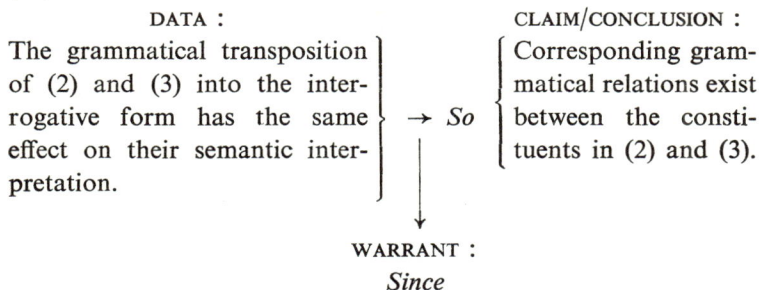

As in the case of (19) Lakoff does not attempt with respect to (22)
to specify its qualifier, conditions of rebuttal, warrant and backing.
The most interesting feature of this argument, however, is the
methodological status of the statement presenting the data. This
statement about the identity of semantic interpretations Lakoff

presents as a protocol sentence. He offers no further arguments in its support. It is therefore justified to conclude that data about the identity or non-identity of semantic interpretations are not hypothetical, but intuitive data. Remarkable, however, is the fact that Lakoff presents in the same paper data about the semantic interpretations of other sentences, (23) and (24), and that these data are clearly regarded by him not as intuitive, but as hypothetical. This is clear from his attempts to demonstrate the correctness of these data by producing further grammatical arguments (cf. Lakoff, 1968: 12).

With respect to (23) and (24) Lakoff states that they differ in their semantic interpretation.

(23)   *The marquis used the knife in order to please his mother*

(24)   *The marquis used the knife in pleasing his mother*

As the data supporting his claim on the non-identity of the semantic interpretations of (23) and (24) Lakoff adduces the statement that (23) and (24) differ with respect to their entailment. Whereas the semantic interpretation of (23) does not entail that the marquis succeeded in pleasing his mother, the semantic interpretation of (24) does entail that the marquis succeeded in pleasing his mother. The warrant in this argument is presumably the following: If the semantic interpretations of two sentences differ with respect to their entailment, then they are non-identical. Schematically this argument can be represented as (25):

(25)

DATA :		CLAIM/CONCLUSION :
The semantic interpretations of (23) and (24) differ with respect to their entailment.	→ *So* ↓	The semantic interpretations of (23) and (24) are non-identical.

WARRANT :

Since

If the semantic interpretations of two sentences
differ with respect to their entailment, then these
semantic interpretations are non-identical.

Notice that Lakoff does not present the data about the difference in entailment of the semantic interpretations of (23) and (24) as intuitive data. He produces a further argument to demonstrate the correctness of the claim about this difference in entailment. This argument he bases on the observation that, whereas (26) is non-deviant, (27) is deviant (p. 12).

(26)   *The marquis used the knife in order to please his mother, but he nevertheless failed to please her*

(27)   **The marquis used the knife in pleasing his mother, but he nevertheless failed to please her*

This argument of Lakoff's can be reconstructed as follows:

(28)

DATA :

(a) The amalgamation of the semantic interpretation of (23) with the semantic interpretation of *but he nevertheless failed to please her* yields a non-deviant amalgam.

(b) The amalgamation of the semantic interpretation of (24) with the semantic interpretation of *but he nevertheless failed to please her* yields a deviant amalgam.

→ So

CLAIM/CONCLUSION :

The semantic interpretations of (23) and (24) differ with respect to their entailment.

WARRANT :

Since

If the amalgamation of the semantic interpretation of a linguistic unit A with respectively the semantic interpretations of the linguistic units B and C yields two semantic amalgams which differ as to their non-deviance, then the semantic interpretations of B and C differ in their entailment.

3.4   THE SECOND MAIN ARGUMENT

In conclusion the argument that Lakoff advances to justify his second grammatical claim, i.e., (15)(ii), will be considered. The claim in this argument is that the deep structure (5), i.e., the deep structure in which the category 'instrumental adverb' is no constituent, must be assigned to sentences (2) and (3). Lakoff presents the data in this argument in terms of the following statements: (a) Should (4), i.e., the deep structure with the constituent 'instrumental adverb', be taken as the deep structure of (2) and (3), it would become necessary to introduce a new selectional restriction into the grammar in order to prevent ungrammatical sentences such as (17)(ii) and (18)(ii) from being characterised as grammatical (cf. Lakoff, 1968: 13-14). There are no independent reasons for introducing this selectional restriction into the grammar. (b) Should (5), i.e., the deep structure without the constituent 'instrumental adverb', be taken as the deep structure of (2) and (3), the generation of ungrammatical sentences such as (17)(ii) and (18)(ii) would be ruled out by a selectional restriction which is already contained by the grammar. The latter selectional restriction — which exists between the verb *use* in the matrix sentence and the verb in the sentence which functions as the complement of *use* — is independently motivated. The warrant in this argument is the following: If the formulation of a structural description requires the postulation of a new selectional restriction which is not needed for independent reasons in the grammar, then this structural description is incorrect and the alternative structural description that is formulated only in terms of independently motivated selectional restrictions is correct. The backing for this warrant is not specified explicitly by Lakoff. It is presumably the following one: Theoretical concepts — such as grammatical categories, grammatical relations and selectional restrictions — which are used in the formulation of structural descriptions must have systematic import. This is to say that these theoretical concepts must occur in more than one grammatical hypothesis with predictive and explanatory power (cf., e.g., Hempel, 1966: 94). This argument can be represented schematically as (29).

(29)

DATA:

CLAIM/CONCLUSION:

(a) Should (4), i.e., the deep structure with the constituent 'instrumental adverb', be taken as the deep structure of (2) and (3), it would become necessary to incorporate a new selectional restriction into the grammar to prevent sentences such as (17) (ii) and (18) (ii) from being characterised as grammatical. This selectional restriction — between the verb and the instrumental adverb — is not needed for independent reasons in the grammar.
(b) Should (5), i.e., the deep structure without the constituent 'instrumental adverb', be taken as the deep structure of (2) and (3), then the generation of ungrammatical sentences such as (17) (ii) and (18) (ii) would be ruled out by a selectional restriction that the grammar contains already. This selectional restriction — between the verb *use* in the matrix sentence and the verb in the sentence functioning as the complement of *use* — is independently motivated.

→ *So*

(5), and not (4), must be taken as the deep structure of the sentences (2) and (3).

WARRANT:
Since
If the formulation of a structural description requires the postulation of a new selectional restriction which is not needed for independent reasons in the grammar, then this structural description is incorrect and the alternative structural description that is formulated only in terms of independently motivated selectional restrictions is correct.

↓

BACKING:
On account of the fact that
Theoretical concepts — such as grammatical categories, grammatical relations and selectional restrictions — which are used in the formulation of structural descriptions must have systematic import.

In (29) it is also the data that are interesting from a methodological point of view. Unlike the data in (16), these data are not hypothetical; unlike the data in (19), they are not intuitive. The data in (29) concern the content of the grammar: (a) the absence or presence of particular theoretical concepts, and (b) the degree to which their incorporation into the grammar is motivated. These data can accordingly be labelled "metatheoretical".

4

THE STRUCTURE OF GRAMMATICAL ARGUMENTATION

4.1 GENERAL REMARKS

A number of the general methodological principles that underlies grammatical argumentation are considered in this section. These principles — which constitute one of the aspects of the structure of grammatical argumentation — determine the form and nature of the grammatical arguments (16), (19), (22), (25), (28), (29) and numerous other similar arguments. It is doubtful whether a grammarian knows these general methodological principles as 'rules' which he can formulate explicitly and justify rationally.[1] The aspect of the structure of grammatical argumentation that will be considered below has a bearing only on the grammatical arguments that are advanced in order to demonstrate the correctness of particular structural descriptions. No attention is given here to the aspect of the structure of grammatical argumentation that underlies arguments for or against the postulation of particular grammatical rules. Although the grammatical arguments which were considered in § 3 concerned only the assignment of deep structures to sentences, it is to be expected that the generalizations about the structure of grammatical argumentation that will be presented below will also be valid for arguments concerning the

---

[1] In his excellent monograph on the structure of scientific revolutions Kuhn (1962: 43 ff.) denies the existence of such rules in empirical science.

other levels of syntactic structure as well as those of phonological and semantic structure.[2]

4.2 GRAMMATICAL PROBLEMS

The first set of general methodological principles that can be abstracted from the grammatical arguments presented in § 3 concerns the nature of grammatical problems. It appears that the existence of Lakoff's major grammatical problem was suggested by an incidental observation: the observation that, despite the differences in their 'syntactic structure', (2) and (3) are semantically interpreted in the same way. The primitive grammatical problem which initiated the grammatical inquiry was accordingly: Why are (2) and (3) semantically synonymous? This fairly primitive grammatical problem is converted into a more sophisticated one by the operation of two sets of factors.

The first aspect of the more sophisticated variant of the primitive problem is determined by the transformational theory of linguistic structure. Since, within the framework of this theory, synonymous sentences, presumably, have the same deep structure this aspect of the more sophisticated problem can be formulated as follows: Do the sentences (2) and (3) have an identical deep structure? The second aspect of the more sophisticated problem is determined by two other observations: (a) that according to the tradition the category 'instrumental adverb' is a constituent of (2), but not of (3), and (b) that this category has been regarded in transformational grammar as a deep structure category and that no motivation has been given for this decision. The second aspect of the more sophisticated problem can be formulated as follows: Do instrumental adverbs occur as a constituent in the deep structure underlying (2), (3) and other similar English sentences?

---

[2] In the published papers on transformational generative semantics few 'semantic' arguments are presented. The patterns of argumentation which Chomsky and Halle (1968) use in phonological analysis are fundamentally similar to those used in syntactic analysis (cf. Botha, in preparation).

The way in which this more sophisticated grammatical problem came into existence lucidly illustrates the point that non-trivial, well-defined grammatical problems exist only within the framework of a specific linguistic theory. The given formulation of the more sophisticated problem derives its significance from the theoretical concepts 'deep structure', 'grammatical category', etc. A first principle with general methodological validity which governs grammatical inquiry is therefore the following: Non-trivial, well-defined grammatical problems exist only within the framework of a particular linguistic theory.

The analysis of the number of grammatical problems presented in § 3 reveals another general methodological feature of grammatical problems: Grammatical problems rarely constitute isolated entities, but tend to be grouped together in series or constellations. Within such a series or constellation grammatical problems are related in a definite, often hierarchic, fashion. For example, the grammatical problem of determining whether (2) and (3) have identical deep structures gives rise to the problem as to whether the constructions in (2) and (3) have relational, selectional, lexical and transformational properties that are in a one-to-one correspondence. Attempts to solve the latter problem, in turn, lead to a further grammatical problem: Do the interrogative structures (20) and (21) have an identical semantic interpretation? In such a fashion grammatical problems form chain-like series.

4.3   GRAMMATICAL WARRANTS

Having defined his grammatical problem as explicitly as possible, the grammarian produces (a) a solution to the problem in the form of a grammatical claim (cf., e.g., (15)(i) and (ii)), (b) data supporting the claim, and (c) a grammatical warrant authorising the step from the data to the claim and, conversely, from the claim to the data. It seems that to the process of constructing grammatical arguments grammatical warrants are, in a certain sense, more fundamental than grammatical data. In order to explicate this statement it is necessary to consider

(i) the way in which the general linguistic theory determines grammatical warrants,

(ii) the structure of grammatical warrants, and

(iii) the logical status of the general linguistic theory and particular grammars.

4.3.1 *The Origin of Grammatical Warrants*

The general linguistic theory, within whose framework the grammarian operates, does not only determine the form and content of the non-trivial grammatical problems, but also defines *a priori* all possible relevant grammatical warrants. These warrants are determined by three aspects of the linguistic theory.

(i) The general linguistic theory specifies the conditions that must be met by each kind of linguistic structure, be it syntactic, phonological or semantic. The transformational theory, for example, stipulates that a structure qualifies as a deep structure only when it meets the conditions (1)(i)-(iv). The conditions on the different levels of linguistic structure determine the first series of warrants that can function in grammatical arguments. For example, the warrant (30), occurring in argument (16), is determined by the conditions (1)(i)-(iv) on deep structure.

(30) If two sentences are constituted by constructions which are in a one-to-one correspondence with respect to relational, selectional, lexical and transformational characteristics, then they have an identical deep structure.

(ii) In addition to the basic conditions on the different types or levels of linguistic structure, exemplified by (1)(i)-(iv), the general linguistic theory also contains auxiliary conditions on these different types of structure. These auxiliary conditions determine a second set of grammatical warrants.

For example, the warrants (31), (32) and (33) which occur respectively in the grammatical arguments (19), (22) and (28), are determined by such auxiliary conditions.

(31)   If the same grammatical modification of two constructions has the same effect on their grammaticalness, then this modification has affected a grammatical characteristic which these constructions share.

(32)   If the same grammatical modification of two sentences has the same effect on their semantic interpretation, then corresponding grammatical relations exist between their constituents.

(33)   If the amalgamation of the semantic interpretation of a linguistic unit A with respectively the semantic interpretations of the linguistic units B and C yields two semantic amalgams which differ as to their non-deviance, then the semantic interpretations of B and C differ in their entailment.

The warrants that can be derived from such auxiliary conditions differ as to their generality — (31) is more generally applicable than either (32) or (33). Some of these warrants are also more general than those considered under (i) above. This is to say that whereas the warrants determined by basic conditions such as (1)(i)-(iv) are usually only applicable at a certain level of linguistic analysis, those determined by auxiliary conditions can often be used in grammatical arguments on different structural levels. Notice, incidentally, the operational nature of the grammatical warrants that are determined by the auxiliary conditions. The linguistic status of these auxiliary conditions is discussed in § 5.3.

(iii) A third set of warrants used in grammatical arguments is determined by the general methodological principles which underlie the transformational theory. The warrant (34), which occurs in the argument (29), is determined by such

a general methodological principle. This general methodological principle is presented as the backing in (29).

(34)   If the formulation of a structural description requires
the postulation of a new selectional restriction which is not
needed for independent reasons in the grammar, then this
structural description is incorrect, and the alternative
structural description that is formulated in terms of independently motivated selectional restrictions is correct.

The warrants that are determined by general methodological
principles can, in principle, function in grammatical arguments on
each of the different structural levels within a grammar. They have
accordingly a wider applicability than the two types of warrants
considered respectively in (i) and (ii) above. Especially the principle of independent motivation is used in grammatical arguments
that have a bearing on the assignment of diverse types of linguistic
structure as well as on the postulation of diverse types of grammatical rules.[3]

4.3.2   *The Internal Structure of Grammatical Warrants*

A grammatical warrant fulfils the function of authorising the
establishment of a link between grammatical data and grammatical
claims by virtue of its internal structure. It has already been
pointed out in § 2 that a warrant is a bridge-like statement that
consists of two components, and has the form: If X, then Y.
Consider, for example, the warrant (35).

(35)

If X,	*then Y*
If the same grammatical relations hold between the constituents of the constructions in two sentences,	then these sentences have an identical deep structure.

The right (= Y) half of a grammatical warrant links up with the
grammatical claim which is offered as the solution to a given

---

[3]   Cf., e.g., Chomsky and Halle, 1968: 48.

grammatical problem. The left (= X) half of a grammatical warrant links up with the data that constitute the base for the claim. Using a grammatical warrant, a grammarian can accordingly depart from a grammatical claim and determine via the left half of the warrant the data that support it, or he can start out from the data and determine via the right half of the warrant the solution to the grammatical problem on which the data have a bearing.

4.3.3   The Logical Status of the General Theory and Particular Grammars

In the introductory subparagraph of § 4.3 it was claimed that to the process of the construction of grammatical arguments, grammatical warrants are, in a certain sense, more fundamental than grammatical data. To make this claim, is to assert that grammatical warrants rather than grammatical data direct the analytical activities of a grammarian. Before this assertion can be explicated fully, the logical status of a general linguistic theory and a particular grammar must still be considered briefly. It has become a commonplace that a grammar is a theory and that a grammarian is occupied with the construction and testing of theories (cf. Bach, 1964: 7; Botha, 1968: 61). The methodological implications of the insight that a grammar is a special kind of theory, a DERIVED or SECONDARY THEORY, have however not been considered fully.

In the normal situation in which grammatical inquiry is conducted, the general linguistic theory exists prior to the grammars that result from its application to the grammatical data. The general linguistic theory accordingly determines the form of the resulting grammars, the non-trivial, well-defined grammatical problems, and the warrants that can be used in grammatical arguments for or against proposed solutions to these grammatical problems. The grammatical warrants are determined by the general linguistic theory even before they are used in concrete grammatical arguments. It seems likely that the relevant grammatical data are usually only determined via the left half of grammatical warrants when these warrants are used in specific grammatical arguments. In this sense grammatical warrants are more fundamental to grammatical inquiry than grammatical data. Notice that the general linguistic theory also indirectly determines the relevant grammatical data via the left half of grammatical warrants.

The fact that a grammar is a secondary or derived theory has another implication, viz. that grammatical arguments are warrant-using arguments. These warrants are supplied by the general linguistic theory, and it follows that linguistic arguments will be warrant-establishing arguments.[4]

4.4 GRAMMATICAL DATA

In this study a distinction has been made between grammatical and linguistic data. When linguistic phenomena are used as data in grammatical arguments, they constitute grammatical data; when they figure in linguistic arguments, they are linguistic data. An analysis of the grammatical arguments considered in § 3 shows that grammatical data belong to three methodologically different types. The first type comprises the intuitive and perceptual judgments native speakers are capable of giving with respect to linguistic utterances. This type of data, that has been labelled 'intuitive data', is presented in terms of protocol sentences such as (36) (cf. argument (19)).

(36)   The replacement of the corresponding verbs in (2) — or (17)(i) — and (3) — or (18)(i) — with verbs which have the selectional feature [— Activity] causes both (2) — or (17)(i) — and (3) — or (18)(i) — to become ungrammatical.

The second type of grammatical data has a hypothetical nature. The correctness of the claims about this type of data must be demonstrated by further grammatical arguments, the last one of

4   For the distinction between warrant-using and warrant-establishing arguments cf. Toulmin, 1964: 135-136.

which must contain non-hypothetical data. The data in argument
(16), that can be presented by the hypothesis (37), are typically
hypothetical.

(37)   The constructions in (2) and (3) have relational, selectional,
        lexical and transformational characteristics which are in
        a one-to-one correspondence.

The third type of grammatical data, i.e., metatheoretical data,
concerns the occurrence of particular theoretical concepts in
grammars as well as the degree of motivation for introducing these
concepts into the grammar. The data in (29), some of which are
presented below as (38), are metatheoretical data.

(38)   Should (5), i.e., the deep structure without the constituent
        'instrumental adverb' be taken as the deep structure of
        (2) and (3), then the generation of ungrammatical sentences
        such as (17)(ii) and (18)(ii) would be ruled out by a selec-
        tional restriction that the grammar contains already. This
        selectional restriction is independently motivated.

The question as to whether particular linguistic phenomena qualify
as relevant grammatical data is decided by considering the content
of the left half of grammatical warrants. The general linguistic
theory determines via the left half of grammatical warrants the
relevant grammatical data. Outside the framework of the transformational theory no principled basis exists for the claim that
the data in argument (16), presented also as (37), are more relevant
to Lakoff's problem than the observation (39).

(39)   Whereas (2) is constituted by only seven 'words', (3) is
        constituted by eight 'words'.

Only within the framework of this theory the data (37) are gram-
matically relevant and significant, and the observation (39) is
irrelevant and insignificant. This fact clearly shows that transformational grammar is no exception to the general methodological 'rule' that in an advanced empirical science systematic
observation is possible only within the framework of an explicitly

outlined theory (cf. Popper, 1964: 46; Hanson, 1965: Chap. 1; Toulmin, 1965: 53ff.). The implication is that a grammarian cannot collect grammatical data in the fashion in which the taxonomic entomologist collects butterflies.

4.5 BACKINGS IN GRAMMATICAL ARGUMENTS

It has already been pointed out in § 4.3.1 that the backings of grammatical warrants are constituted by the theoretical and methodological principles of the general linguistic theory. Grammarians often do not present explicitly the backings in their arguments. The task of demonstrating the correctness of these backings is taken to be that of the linguist and not that of the grammarian. Grammarians usually treat their grammatical warrants as if they were supported by correct backings. This, of course, does not imply that these backings are in fact correct.

4.6 PATTERNS OF GRAMMATICAL ARGUMENTS

The relations between the grammatical arguments that a grammarian uses in a particular grammatical analysis are of two basic types These grammatical arguments are either in a complementary or in a supplementary relation to each other.

Transformational grammarians such as Lakoff attach much value to the principle of independent argumentation (cf. (29)). Before a (new) grammatical concept — such as a particular selectional restriction or grammatical category — can be used in the formulation of a given structural description, it must be shown that this concept is also needed for other, independent reasons in the grammar. This condition roughly implies that the given concept must also be needed for the solution of grammatical problems other than the one which is the immediate concern of the grammarian. It is assumed that the more independent grammatical arguments can be provided for the introduction of a given grammatical concept, the better motivated is the step of introducing this concept. The diverse grammatical arguments which are given to justify the introduction of a particular grammatical concept are in a complementary relation to each other. This is the first way in which a number of related grammatical arguments can be patterned.

The grammatical arguments that are used in a particular grammatical analysis can also be related in a non-complementary way. When the data in a given grammatical argument have a hypothetical nature, further grammatical arguments are needed to demonstrate the correctness of the claims about these data (cf. (19)). These further arguments, in turn, may also incorporate grammatical data which are hypothetical. Still more arguments will then be required to justify the claims about the hypothetical data which occur in the latter arguments. In this way grammatical arguments are grouped together to form a chain-like, linearly ordered series. The grammatical arguments (22), (25) and (28) constitute such a series. The arguments in such a series are related in two ways: supplementarily and hierarchically. This is the second way in which related arguments can be patterned. Only an argument whose data are non-hypothetical can terminate such a series of arguments. An argument with hypothetical data can never conclude it, because the correctness of the claims about these data is not evident on *a priori* grounds.[5]

4.7 SUMMARY OF CONCLUSIONS

The conclusions about the structure of grammatical argumentation that were drawn in §§ 4.1-4.6 are provisional. A more extensive analysis of grammatical arguments will undoubtedly reveal that these conclusions are incorrect in certain respects and incomplete

---

[5] The fact that intuitive and perceptual data can occur in an argument which terminates a series of supplementary arguments constitutes a good reason to call these data 'primary data'.

in others. At this point these conclusions may be summarised in the following way:

(i) The existence of grammatical problems is often indicated by incidental observations. The non-trivial, well-defined versions of grammatical problems are, however, determined by the general linguistic theory within the framework of which the grammarian operates.

(ii) The possible hypothetical claims that grammarians offer as solutions to grammatical problems are also determined by the general linguistic theory via the right half of grammatical warrants.

(iii) The grammarian derives the warrants in his grammatical arguments from three sources in the general linguistic theory: (a) the basic conditions on the different types of linguistic structure, (b) the more general auxiliary conditions on these types of linguistic structure, and (c) the general methodological principles underlying the linguistic theory.

(iv) These conditions and principles constitute the linguistic backings of the grammatical warrants.

(v) Via the left half of the grammatical warrants the general linguistic theory also determines the possible relevant grammatical data.

(vi) The grammatical data belong to three methodologically different types: intuitive or perceptual, hypothetical, and metatheoretical.

(vii) In the case of grammatical arguments that contain hypothetical data, further arguments must be provided to demonstrate the correctness of the claims about the hypothetical data. These further arguments form series of which the constituents bear hierarchical, supplementary relations to each other.

(viii) To satisfy the methodological condition of independent argumentation, more than one unrelated argument must be provided to justify a (new) grammatical concept. These arguments form clusters whose constituents bear a complementary relation to each other.

GRAMMATICAL ARGUMENTATION AS A SOLUTION TO THE CONFIRMATION PROBLEM

5.1 GENERAL REMARKS

In § 1.2 it was shown that a grammarian who assigns a specific structural description SD_1 to a specific sentence S at a particular level of linguistic structure L, must demonstrate why SD_1, and not one of the other theoretically conceivable structural descriptions SD_2.,.., SD_x, must be assigned to S at L. This task constitutes one aspect of the grammatical confirmation problem. The question now is whether grammatical argumentation is a methodologically valid solution to this problem (cf. § 1.4).

Before discussing the latter question a clear distinction must be made between:

    (i) the validity of the general methodological principles that underlie grammatical argumentation, and

    (ii) the degree of perfection to which these principles are applied in actual cases of grammatical analysis by an arbitrary grammarian.

It is necessary to make this distinction, since, obviously, grammarians can use the methodological principles of grammatical argumentation in an imperfect way. For example, arguments without warrants or backings may be provided, arguments with irrelevant data may be advanced, etc. On these 'performance' flaws in grammatical arguments no further comments will be made. Only the question of the general validity of grammatical argumentation as a solution to the grammatical confirmation problem will be considered.

It will be maintained that grammatical argumentation is at present for two sets of reasons an unacceptable solution to the grammatical confirmation problem. The first set of reasons concerns the obscurity of a number of the fundamental methodological principles of grammatical argumentation. The second set of reasons has a bearing on the failure of grammatical argumentation to confront grammatical claims with independent, true data.

5.2 OBSCURITY OF FUNDAMENTAL METHODOLOGICAL PRINCIPLES

5.2.1 *The Principle of Independent Argumentation*

Several aspects of the principle of independent argumentation, as it is used by grammarians who operate within the framework of transformational grammar, are obscure.

In the first place, the precise contents that the notion of independence has in the context of grammatical analysis has, to my knowledge, not been specified and justified explicitly by grammarians who use it. At present no non-arbitrary answer can accordingly be given to the question as to whether two grammarical arguments, GA_1 and GA_2, are 'independent' of each other. The formulation of this principle in terms of the concept 'systematic import' in (29) is nothing but the result of some guessing on my part. Specifying and justifying the content of this concept is a non-trivial undertaking.

In the second place, I have failed to find in transformationalist writings an answer to the question as to why a principle of independent argumentation should be used at all by a grammarian. Philosophers of science such as Nagel (1961: 147) and Hempel (1966: 94) consider independent motivation as a general methodological condition on concept formation in empirical science in general. Chomsky and Halle (1965: 111), however, do not accept every general methodological principle of empirical science in general as also valid in transformational generative grammar. For example, they are unwilling to use a general criterion of simplicity in transformational grammar, since the relevance of such a criterion to this theory has not been demonstrated. If we grant them this point, it is only reasonable to expect that the relevance of a general methodological principle of independent argumentation to transformational grammar must also be explicitly shown. To my knowledge this has not yet been done.

In the third place, it is unclear precisely what the limits of the range of applicability of the criterion of independent argumentation is in transformational grammar. Furthermore, the way in which these limits are determined is obscure. This criterion is, for example, used in grammatical arguments that are advanced to motivate structural descriptions at the level of deep structure. It is however set aside by Chomsky and Halle (1968: 44ff., 145ff., 298) as a condition that must be met by the structural descriptions at the level of lexical phonological representation.[1] It is not clear on the basis of which methodological or linguistic considerations the range of applicability of this criterion is determined. It is accordingly impossible to assess the validity of these considerations.

5.2.2   *The Power of Individual Arguments and of Sets of Arguments*

No explicit answer has yet been given to the question as to whether all grammatical arguments have the same power or whether different types of arguments are not equally powerful. This question becomes acute when alternative, competing solutions to a given grammatical problem can be provided, and when each of the alternative solutions is supported by grammatical arguments. In such a situation the grammarian must, firstly, determine the power of each individual argument. Secondly, he must determine

---

[1]   This point is discussed further in Botha, in preparation: § 5. 2. 3. 2. 4. 5.

the collective power of each of the sets of arguments that support the alternative solutions. To my knowledge no measure for determining the power of individual grammatical arguments and that of sets of arguments has been provided. This implies that decisions on the power of individual arguments and sets of arguments are at present made either in an intuitive way or in a downright arbitrary fashion.

5.2.3 *Grammatical Argumentation and the Evaluation Measure*

Another obscure aspect of grammatical argumentation concerns its relation to the evaluation measure that the transformational generative theory provides for selecting the most highly valued grammar from the alternative grammars for the same language. According to Chomsky and Halle (1968: 330-331) it is possible to construct within the framework of this general linguistic theory alternative, competing grammars for the same natural language. None of these competing grammars need be in conflict with the available grammatical data about this language. The general linguistic theory accordingly provides an evaluation measure for selecting the best one of the competing grammars. Chomsky and Halle (1968: 330-331; 1965: 107, 108, 109) take great pains to stress the point that this evaluation measure is an empirical one, i.e., one that can be proved to be correct or incorrect.[2]

A grammarian who operates within the framework of transformational generative grammar has therefore at his disposal two different procedures that can be followed to determine which one of a number of competing grammatical analyses is the best: grammatical argumentation and the evaluation measure.[3] Grammatical argumentation can be used in the phase of constructing grammars, i.e., in the pretheoretical phase of grammatical inquiry. It is based

[2] For a discussion of the question whether the evaluation measure is in fact an empirical measure cf. Botha, 1970: § 6.3.1, and Botha, in preparation: § § 4.3.3.5.2., 4.3.3.5.4., 5.2.2.2.
[3] The third possible procedure, viz. the testing of the predictions of the rules which generate the structural descriptions, is for the moment not taken into consideration (cf. § 1.2).

on principles that have not yet been illustrated as being empirical within the framework of transformational grammar. The evaluation measure, in turn, can be used in the phase of testing grammars, i.e., in the theoretical phase of grammatical inquiry. Since both of these procedures have the function of restricting the arbitrariness of grammatical analyses, the following questions arise: In what way are these procedures related? Must they be regarded as supplementary, complementary, alternative, or conflicting procedures?

To make sure that a glaring inconsistency is not incorporated into the methodological basis of transformational generative grammar, these questions must be answered in a satisfactory way. This inconsistency consists in the fact that grammatical argumentation determines the members of the set of alternative grammars from which the most highly valued one must be selected by the evaluation measure. Whereas the empirical nature of the evaluation measure is demonstrated, according to Chomsky and Halle, beyond doubt, the empirical status of grammatical argumentation has not been established in the context of transformational generative grammar. Since grammatical argumentation functions in the overall process of grammatical inquiry before the evaluation measure, its non-empirical nature neutralises the empirical status of the evaluation measure. It is absurd to attempt to select in an empirical way the most highly valued grammar from a set of alternative grammars whose membership is regulated by a principle of which the empirical status has not been established.

5.2.4 *Intuitive vs. Hypothetical Data*

The distinction between intuitive and hypothetical data is not sufficiently clear. In § 3 it was found that, whereas data about the identity of semantic interpretations are in some cases presented as intuitive data (cf. (22)), such data are presented in other cases as hypothetical data (cf. (25)). Furthermore, whereas data about the identity of semantic interpretations are presented in (25) as hypothetical data, data about the deviance of semantic interpretations are presented in (28) as intuitive data. The basis on which it is decided whether data are intuitive or hypothetical cannot be abstracted from the arguments (22), (25) and (28). To my knowledge it has not yet been specified and motivated explicitly.

It is of the utmost importance that a grammarian who regards grammatical argumentation as a solution to the confirmation problem should use a principled criterion for distinguishing between intuitive and hypothetical data. It would be senseless to provide grammatical arguments in justification of a given grammatical claim without knowing whether the data in these arguments were intuitive or hypothetical. Should these data be hypothetical, further arguments would be needed to establish their correctness. Should the grammarian have failed to recognise these data as hypothetical and should he, therefore, have failed to establish their correctness by means of further arguments, his using a grammatical argument in the first place to justify the original grammatical claim would be pointless.

5.2.5   *Summary of Conclusions*

A first reason for not accepting grammatical argumentation as a methodologically valid solution to the grammatical confirmation problem is that, at least, the following of its aspects are obscure:

   (i) the motivation for using a principle of independent argumentation at all in transformational grammar;

  (ii) the precise content of the notion of independence in terms of which this principle is formulated;

 (iii) the range of applicability of the principle of independent argumentation;

 (iv) the measure for determining the power of a grammatical argument with respect to that of other grammatical arguments;

  (v) the measure for determining the combined power of a set of complementary arguments;

(vi) the relation between grammatical argumentation, as a procedure whose empirical status is unclear, and the evaluation
measure, which is an empirical measure;

(vii) the precise way in which the distinction between hypothetical and intuitive data is drawn.

5.3   THE STATUS OF GRAMMATICAL WARRANTS

From the way in which the concepts 'confirmation' and 'dis-
confirmation' are characterised in § 1.2 it follows that a proposed
confirmation procedure must satisfy a specific condition of adequacy. It must be possible by means of such a procedure to check
the correctness of a claim against independent evidence, i.e.
evidence of which the correctness has already been established at
an intersubjective level. Grammatical argumentation can be
considered a valid confirmation procedure if it is known on
independent grounds that

(i) the data in grammatical arguments are correct, and

(ii) the grammatical warrants are generally valid, i.e., that their
linguistic backings are true.

This condition has already been mentioned in § 2 in the discussion
of the distinction between well-formed arguments with true
conclusions and well-formed arguments with false conclusions.

Consider first the general validity of grammatical warrants.
A grammatical warrant can be taken to be generally valid if it is
derived from a correct general linguistic principle. Every linguist
who has more than a superficial knowledge of transformational
generative grammar knows of how preciously few general linguistic
principles the correctness has been established beyond all doubt.
Literally in each major paper on the theoretical fundamentals of
transformational generative grammar the correctness of one or
more of its theoretical principles is questioned. Many recent
publications support this claim. Consider, for example, the way
in which Chomsky and Halle find some of the most fundamental

principles of phonology inadequate in Chapter 9 of *The Sound Pattern of English*.[4] Consider also the way in which Fillmore finds the organisation of the base component unsatisfactory in his paper *The Case for Case,* as well as the way in which Seuren proposes a drastically modified version of the base component in his monograph *Operators and Nucleus : A Contribution to the Theory of Grammar*.[5] I have the idea that a stocktaking of the theoretical principles whose correctness has been established beyond all doubt, will yield meagre results. This dynamic development of transformational grammar is typical of a science which is still in a revolutionary phase (cf. Kuhn, 1962: 76, 90).

Notice furthermore that in some grammatical arguments that are provided by respectable transformationalists such as Lakoff, warrants are used which are derived from obscure theoretical principles. The warrants (31), (32) and (33) occurring respectively in the arguments (19), (22) and (28) are typical examples of warrants that are based on auxiliary theoretical principles that have not yet been articulated fully and motivated explicitly. Arguments that contain warrants derived from such auxiliary theoretical principles lack all confirmatory power.

Consider secondly the correctness of the statements that present the data in grammatical arguments. It has been pointed out that a grammarian must prove the correctness of hypothetical data by providing further grammatical arguments. It is possible that in the latter arguments warrants occur which do not have general linguistic backings whose correctness has been proved. Argument (28) is a case in point. The implication is that not even the correctness of the data in some grammatical arguments is beyond doubt.

The conclusion must be that grammatical argumentation within the framework of transformational generative grammar is also for a second reason an unacceptable solution to the grammatical confirmation problem. It fails as a confirmation procedure, since the correctness of the linguistic backings and grammatical data of

[4] Cf. also Postal, 1968: 65ff.
[5] Cf. also the alternative conceptions of the base component proposed by Bach (1968) and McCawley (1968).

too many arguments has not been established on the basis of independent, correct evidence. Clearly an argumentation procedure such as grammatical argumentation cannot be an adequate confirmation procedure in a science that has not progressed beyond the revolutionary stage of development. The conditions of adequacy for such a procedure — viz. that the correctness of the backings and data in arguments must have been established on independent grounds — cannot be met in a science which is in a revolutionary phase of development.[6] Notice that in the approach to the confirmation problem in terms of the formulation of explicit grammatical rules and the checking of the correctness of their predictions grammarians need not depart from the, counter to fact, assumption that the principles of the general linguistic theory are correct beyond all doubt.

Grammatical argumentation may even influence the empirical status of grammars in a negative way. If a grammarian is exclusively occupied with constructing grammatical arguments for or against particular structural descriptions, he obviously does not proceed to the stage of grammatical inquiry in which explicit grammatical rules are formulated. Firstly, this fact has a negative effect on the explicitness of grammars. Secondly, it precludes the use of the second approach to the grammatical confirmation problem, viz. testing the correctness of the predictions of grammatical rules.

[6]   To my mind no present-day theory of linguistic structure can meet these conditions.

GRAMMATICAL ARGUMENTATION AS SUSTENANCE AND HEURISTIC PROCEDURE

6.1 GENERAL REMARKS

The question now is whether grammatical argumentation, failing to qualify as a confirmation procedure, has at all a useful methodological function within the framework of transformational generative grammar. The answer to this question is that it has two extremely useful functions, the functions of sustenance and heuristic procedure.

6.2 GRAMMATICAL ARGUMENTATION AS SUSTENANCE PROCEDURE

According to Bunge (1959: 78ff.), a distinction must be made between the sustenance and the confirmation of a theory or hypothesis. As has been pointed out, hypotheses are confirmed or disconfirmed by testing the correctness of their consequences against independent evidence. However, before hypotheses are tested in this way, they already have a certain degree of probability. This is due to the fact that hypotheses or theories are not built *ex nihilo* but rest on certain bases which support them before and after they have been tested in the way mentioned above. These bases that support hypotheses or theories before and after they have been tested, constitute their SUSTENANCE.

Both scientific and non-scientific data can be used as the sustenance of hypotheses. The scientific data can be either EMPIRICAL or RATIONAL, the non-scientific data either PSYCHOLOGICAL or CULTURAL (cf. Bunge, 1959: 78ff.). The nature of the latter two kinds of sustenance, related respectively to aesthetic or 'logical' feelings and a prevailing *Zeitgeist,* will not be commented on further. The empirical sustenance of a theory is constituted by true experiential evidence about the objects to which the theory refers. For example, the neurophysiological evidence about the finiteness of a human being's immediate memory can be regarded as the empirical sustenance of the transformationalist hypothesis that the lexicon of a grammar consists of a FINITE set of entries and redundancy rules (cf. Katz, 1967: 174). The support that a theory receives from other theories or hypotheses with which it is consistent constitutes its rational sustenance. Rational sustenance does not have the experiential nature of empirical sustenance and concerns the question as to how well a theory or hypothesis fits into an already existing theoretical frame.

The first useful methodological function of grammatical argumentation is that it provides the rational sustenance of proposed structural descriptions. Grammatical arguments give, on rational grounds, some grammatical claims a higher degree of probability than others. It therefore restricts, in a rational way, the arbitrariness of structural descriptions. The sustenance provided by grammatical argumentation is rational and not empirical, since the validity of the grammatical warrants in the most arguments has not been established on experiential grounds. Grammatical argumentation shows that some structural descriptions are within the framework of the general linguistic theory more probable than others. In the cases in which the correctness of grammatical data and the validity of grammatical warrants have been established on experiential grounds, grammatical arguments provide the empirical sustenance of grammatical hypotheses. If the term 'confirmation procedure' is restricted to the approach of testing the correctness of grammars by means of checking the accuracy of their predictions, grammatical argumentation as a sustenance procedure can be taken as complementing this confirmation procedure. The usefulness of grammatical argumentation as a sustenance proce-

dure is however also limited by the obscurity of some of its fundamental methodological principles (cf. § 5.2).

6.3 GRAMMATICAL ARGUMENTATION AS HEURISTIC PROCEDURE

The second useful methodological function of grammatical argumentation is that of heuristic procedure. It has this function by
virtue of the heuristic power of grammatical warrants. In § 4.3.2
it was pointed out that grammatical warrants are binarily struc-
tured: the left half linking up with grammatical data and the right
half linking up with grammatical claims. A grammatical warrant
accordingly has heuristic power that can be applied in two direc-
tions: from left to right and from right to left.

The grammarian who has in the form of a grammatical claim
a hypothetical solution to a grammatical problem can use the left
half of the grammatical warrant, whose right half links up with
the given claim, to determine the data that will support the claim.
For example, the left half of the warrant (30) occurring in argument (16) suggests that the data that will support the claim in
(16) are constituted by relational, selectional, transformational and
lexical characteristics of the constructions in (2) and (3). This
example illustrates the heuristic power that a grammatical warrant
has when applied from right to left.

A grammarian who has made a number of observations that
needs an explanation can use the right half of the grammatical
warrant, whose left half links up with these data, to determine
this explanation. For example, the right half of the grammatical
warrant (40) suggests an explanation for the observation that (2)
and (3) are synonymous.

(40)   If two sentences are synonymous, then they presumably
        have an identical deep structure.[1]

---

[1] The modal expression "presumably" must be incorporated into (40),
since sentences that are paraphrases of each other are semantically synonymous
without having an identical deep structure.

This example illustrates the heuristic power that a grammatical warrant can have when applied from left to right.

Note that it is not claimed that grammatical argumentation constitutes a MECHANICAL heuristic procedure. In other words, it is not claimed that a computer equipped with a program of grammatical warrants will be able to assign to an arbitrary sentence the correct structural description.

In conclusion it must be pointed out that under certain circumstances the use of grammatical argumentation may also have negative consequences for the overall process of grammatical inquiry. This is the case when the grammarian is to such an extent preoccupied with the task of finding grammatical arguments for or against structural descriptions and grammatical rules that he fails to proceed to the stage in grammatical inquiry in which the grammatical rules are formalised. In Chomsky and Halle's monograph *The Sound Pattern of English* it is made abundantly clear that formalisation has a twofold function. Firstly, it constitutes the means by which grammatical rules are formulated in their simplest and most explicit form. Secondly, formalisation has a heuristic function (cf. Chomsky and Halle, 1968: 333). Some of the notational conventions in terms of which rules are formalised have empirical consequences for their ordering with respect to each other. For example, the notational convention governing the use of braces, { }, specifies that partly identical rules must be abbreviated by placing their corresponding non-identical parts in braces. In terms of this convention the partly identical phonological rules (41)(i)-(iv) must be abbreviated to the rule schema (42) (cf. Chomsky and Halle, 1968: 333).

(41)   (i)   i → y / — p
         (ii)   i → y / — r
         (iii) i → y / — y
         (iv)   i → y / — a

(42)

$$i \rightarrow y / - \begin{Bmatrix} p \\ r \\ y \\ a \end{Bmatrix}$$

The rule schema (42) contains the implicit empirical claim that the partly identical rules (41)(i)-(iv) follow immediately on each other in a disjunctively ordered linear series. This claim illustrates the heuristic power of the conventions governing the use of braces. A grammarian who does not proceed to the stage of formalising rules, because he is predominantly occupied with providing grammatical arguments for or against structural descriptions and unformalised rules, cannot exploit the heuristic power of formalisation. This is the sense in which an unbalanced preoccupation with grammatical argumentation may arrest progress in grammatical inquiry.

7

SUMMARY OF MAJOR CONCLUSIONS

(i) A number of the most fundamental methodological principles underlying grammatical analysis are obscure.

(ii) Grammatical argumentation fails to qualify as a confirmation procedure, since
 (a) the correctness of the general linguistic backings of grammatical warrants has not been proved, and
 (b) the correctness of many claims about hypothetical data cannot be established beyond doubt.

(iii) Grammatical argumentation is a useful procedure of inquiry, since
 (a) it provides the rational sustenance of grammatical claims, and
 (b) it has heuristic power.

BIBLIOGRAPHY

Bach, Emmon
    1964   *An Introduction to Transformational Grammars* (New York).
    1968   "Nouns and Noun Phrases", in Bach and Harms (eds.) (1968), 91-122.
Bach, Emmon, and Robert T. Harms (eds.)
    1968   *Universals in Linguistic Theory* (New York).
Botha, Rudolf P.
    1968   *The Function of the Lexicon in Transformational Generative Grammar* (= *Janua Linguarum,* series maior 38), (The Hague and Paris).
    1970   "Methodologische Aspecten van de Transformationeel-Generatieve Fonologie", *Studia Neerlandica* 1, 1.
    in preparation *Methodological Aspects of Transformational Generative Phonology* (= *Janua Linguarum,* series minor), (The Hague and Paris).
Bunge, Mario
    1959   *Metascientific Queries* (Springfield, Ill.).
Caws, Peter
    1965   *The Philosophy of Science: A Systematic Account* (Princeton).
Chomsky, Noam
    1957   *Syntactic Structures* (= *Janua Linguarum,* series minor 4), (The Hague and Paris).
    1965   *Aspects of the Theory of Syntax* (Cambridge, Mass.).
Chomsky, Noam, and Morris Halle
    1965   "Some Controversial Questions in Phonological Theory", *Journal of Linguistics* 1, 97-138.
    1968   *The Sound Pattern of English* (New York).
Clark, Romane, and Paul Welsch
    1962   *Introduction to Logic* (Princeton).
Fillmore, Charles J.
    1968   "The Case for Case", in Bach and Harms (eds.) (1968), 1-88.
Fodor, Jerry A., and Jerrold J. Katz (eds.)
    1964   *The Structure of Language: Readings in the Philosophy of Language* (Englewood Cliffs, N.J.).
Hanson, Norwood Russel
    1965   *Patterns of Discovery* (Cambridge).

Hempel, Carl G.
    1965   *Aspects of Scientific Explanation: And Other Essays in the Philosophy of Science* (New York).
    1966   *Philosophy of Natural Science* (Englewood Cliffs, N.J.).
Jacobs, Roderick, and Peter S. Rosenbaum (eds.)
    in press   *Readings in English Transformational Grammar* (Waltham, Mass.).
Katz, Jerrold J.
    1964a   "Semi-sentences", in Fodor and Katz (eds.) (1964), 400-416.
    1964b   "Mentalism in Linguistics", *Language* 40, 124-137.
    1967   "Recent Issues in Semantic Theory", *Foundations of Language* 3, 124-194.
Katz, Jerrold J., and Paul M. Postal
    1964   *An Integrated Theory of Linguistic Descriptions* (Cambridge, Mass.).
Kuhn, Thomas S.
    1962   *The Structure of Scientific Revolutions* (Chicago and London).
Lakoff, George
    1968   "Instrumental Adverbs and the Concept of Deep Structure", *Foundations of Language* 4, 4-29.
Lees, Robert B.
    1959   *The Grammar of English Nominalizations* (Bloomington and The Hague).
McCawley, James D.
    1968   "The Role of Semantics in Grammar", in Bach and Harms (eds.) (1968), 125-169.
Nagel, Ernest
    1961   *The Structure of Science: Problems in the Logic of Scientific Explanation* (London).
Popper, Karl R.
    1964   *Conjectures and Refutations: The Growth of Scientific Knowledge* (London).
Postal, Paul M.
    1968   *Aspects of Phonological Theory* (New York, Evanston, and London).
Ross, John Robert
    in press   "On Declarative Sentences", in Jacobs and Rosenbaum (eds.), in press.
Salmon, Wesley C.
    1963   *Logic* (Englewood Cliffs, N.J.).
Seuren, P.A.M.
    1969   *Operators and Nucleus: A Contribution to the Theory of Grammar* (Cambridge).
Toulmin, Stephen E.
    1964   "The Layout of Arguments", in *The Uses of Argument* (Cambridge).
    1965   *The Philosophy of Science: An Introduction* (7th Printing) (London).

INDEX